GO QUIZ YOURSELF ON
SPACE

IZZI HOWELL

CRABTREE
PUBLISHING COMPANY
WWW.CRABTREEBOOKS.COM

T0009923

CRABTREE

PUBLISHING COMPANY
WWW.CRABTREEBOOKS.COM

Author: Izzi Howell
Editorial director: Kathy Middleton
Series editor: Izzi Howell
Editor: Crystal Sikkens
Proofreader: Wendy Scavuzzo
Series design: Rocket Design (East Anglia) Ltd
Prepress technician: Katherine Berti
Print coordinator: Katherine Berti

Every effort has been made to clear copyright.
Should there be any inadvertent omission,
please apply to the publisher for rectification.

The website addresses (URLs) included in this book were
valid at the time of going to press. However, it is possible that
contents or addresses may have changed since the publication
of this book. No responsibility for any such changes can be
accepted by either the author or the publisher.

All facts and statistics were correct at the time of press.

Picture acknowledgements: Getty: normaals 8–9b;
Shutterstock: (cover) Alexander Ryabintsev tl, Alabama
Dream tr, Sunnydream c, Cube29 bl, puruan br, ONYXprj
3, 4–5, 10–11 and 29, SkyPics Studio 5t, 13, 21t, peiyang 6tl,
Meowu 6tc and 9c, MightyRabittCrew 6tr and 38t, Transia
Design 7tl, pixbox77 7tc, codesyn 7tr, bhjary 9t, EgudinKa
12t, 20 and 21br, Aphelleon 14, shooarts 15t and 16–17,
BigMouse 15b, Sea Owl 18t and 22–23, mapichai 18b,
Natali Snailcat and Panda Vector 19t, moremari 19b, Dotted
Yeti 21bl, VectorMine 24–25, 26, 27t and 36–37, Nasky
25b, fluidworkshop 27b, pashabo 30t, Nevada31 30–31b,
Carolina K. Smith MD 31t, FrimuFilms 32b, HelenField 34–35,
Quarta 37b, vectortatu 38b, kotoffei 39b, NeutronStar8
40–41, 42c and 46–47, Musjaka 42b, graphic-line 43t, Blan-k
43b; NASA: 33b, NASA, ESA, and S. Beckwith (STScI) and
the HUDF Team 39t, Event Horizon Telescope Collaboration
42t. All design elements from Shutterstock.

Library and Archives Canada Cataloguing in Publication

Title: Go quiz yourself on space / Izzi Howell.
Other titles: Space
Names: Howell, Izzi, author.
Description: Series statement: Go quiz yourself | Includes
 index.
Identifiers: Canadiana (print) 20200358634 | Canadiana
 (ebook) 20200358715 | ISBN 9781427128744
 (hardcover) | ISBN 9781427128805 (softcover) | ISBN
 9781427128867 (HTML)
Subjects: LCSH: Astronomy—Juvenile literature. | LCSH:
 Astronomy—Problems, exercises, etc.—Juvenile
 literature.
Classification: LCC QB46 .H69 2021 | DDC j520—dc23

Library of Congress Cataloging-in-Publication Data

Library of Congress Cataloging-in-Publication Data

Names: Howell, Izzi, author.
Title: Go quiz yourself on space / Izzi Howell.
Description: New York, NY : Crabtree Publishing Company,
 2021. | Series: Go quiz yourself | Includes index. | Audience:
 Ages 9–14+ | Audience: Grades 4-6 | Summary: "Read
 all about our incredible universe, mysterious planets,
 exploding stars, brave astronauts, powerful rockets,
 and much more. Then see if you can answer questions,
 such as: Why does Mars look red? On which planet do
 clouds smell like rotten eggs? Who was the first living
 thing to orbit Earth?"-- Provided by publisher.
Identifiers: LCCN 2020046071 (print) |
 LCCN 2020046072 (ebook) |
 ISBN 9781427128744 (hardcover) |
 ISBN 9781427128805 (paperback) |
 ISBN 9781427128867 (ebook)
Subjects: LCSH: Astronomy--Juvenile literature. |
 Astronomy-- Problems, exercises, etc.--Juvenile literature.
Classification: LCC QB46 .H69 2021 (print) |
 LCC QB46 (ebook) | DDC 520--dc23
LC record available at https://lccn.loc.gov/2020046071
LC ebook record available at https://lccn.loc.gov/2020046072

Crabtree Publishing Company

www.crabtreebooks.com   1–800–387–7650

Published by Crabtree Publishing Company in 2021

First published in Great Britain in 2020 by Wayland
Copyright ©Hodder and Stoughton Limited, 2020

**Published
in Canada
Crabtree Publishing**
616 Welland Ave.
St. Catharines, Ontario
L2M 5V6

**Published in
the United States
Crabtree Publishing**
347 Fifth Ave
Suite 1402-145
New York, NY 10016

Printed in the U.S.A./122020/CG20201014

CONTENTS

HOW TO USE THIS BOOK

This book is packed full of amazing facts and statistics. After you've finished reading a section, test yourself with questions on the following pages. Check your answers on pages 44-45 and see if you're a quizmaster or if you need to quiz it again! When you've finished, test your friends and family to find out who's the ultimate quiz champion!

SPACE

Space is made up of many stars, solar systems, and galaxies. Our planet, Earth, is located in a solar system made up of eight planets and many other objects, all of which orbit the Sun.

ORBITS

The Sun is at the center of our solar system. It is so large that its **gravity** (the force that pulls objects toward each other) pulls the planets and other objects into orbit around it. They orbit around the Sun in circular or oval-shaped paths.

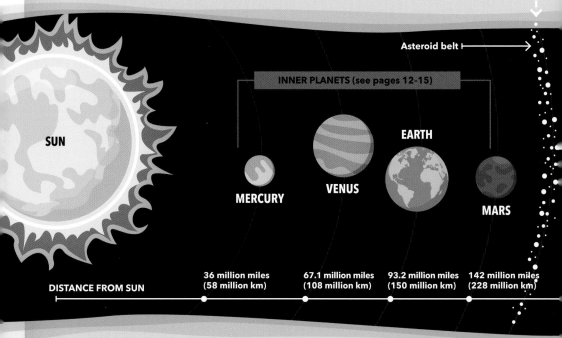

Asteroid belt

INNER PLANETS (see pages 12–15)

SUN

MERCURY

VENUS

EARTH

MARS

DISTANCE FROM SUN

| | 36 million miles (58 million km) | 67.1 million miles (108 million km) | 93.2 million miles (150 million km) | 142 million miles (228 million km) |

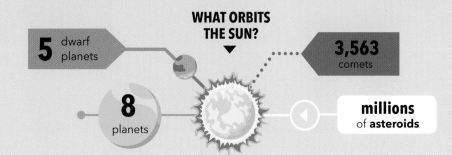

WHAT ORBITS THE SUN?
▼

5 dwarf planets

8 planets

3,563 comets

millions of **asteroids**

ASTEROIDS

Asteroids are large space rocks that orbit the Sun. They are too small to be considered planets or **dwarf planets**. Most of the asteroids in our solar system are found in an asteroid belt between Mars and Jupiter (see pages 18–19).

Since 2006, Pluto has been classified as a dwarf planet. Dwarf planets are round objects that orbit the Sun. They are smaller than planets, but don't have enough gravity to clear their orbit path of smaller objects.

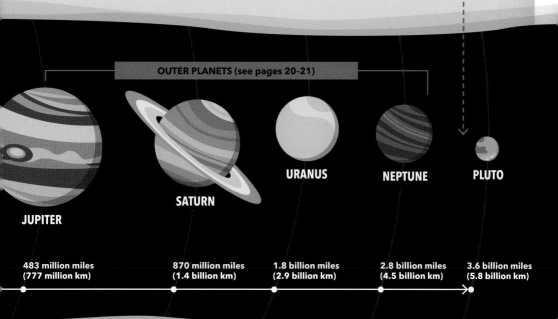

OUTER PLANETS (see pages 20–21)

URANUS

SATURN

NEPTUNE

PLUTO

JUPITER

| 483 million miles (777 million km) | 870 million miles (1.4 billion km) | 1.8 billion miles (2.9 billion km) | 2.8 billion miles (4.5 billion km) | 3.6 billion miles (5.8 billion km) |

PLANET YEARS

One orbit around the Sun is known as a year. On Earth, a year lasts 365.25 days. Planets and objects that are farther from the Sun take longer to orbit, so their years are much longer.

MERCURY: 88 days

VENUS: 225 days

MARS: 687 days

JUPITER: 4,333 days

SATURN: 10,759 days

URANUS: 30,687 days

NEPTUNE: 60,190 days

THE UNIVERSE

The universe contains the whole of space. It's made up of everything that exists, including our solar system, as well as countless stars, galaxies, and planets. It's almost impossible for us to understand the massive size of the universe.

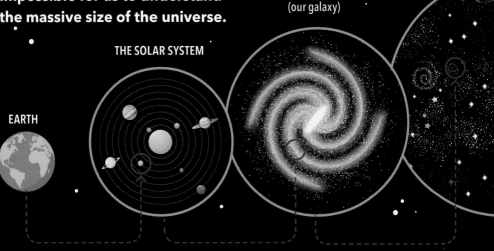

THE LOCAL GROUP
(the **cluster** of galaxies where the Milky Way is located)

THE MILKY WAY
(our galaxy)

THE SOLAR SYSTEM

EARTH

MEASURING DISTANCES

Many objects in the universe are so far away that measuring distances with miles or kilometers would give us ridiculously huge numbers that would be hard to work with. Instead, we measure distances using astronomical units (AU). One AU is 92,955,807 miles (149,597,871 km)—the average distance from Earth to the Sun.

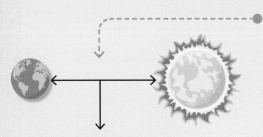

**92,955,807 miles
(149,597,871 km)
or 1 AU**

LIGHT YEARS

Light years are an even larger unit of distance, used for objects far outside of our solar system. Light is the fastest moving thing in the universe. One light year is the distance traveled by light in one Earth year. It's equivalent to 63,240 AU or around 5.9 trillion miles (9.5 trillion km).

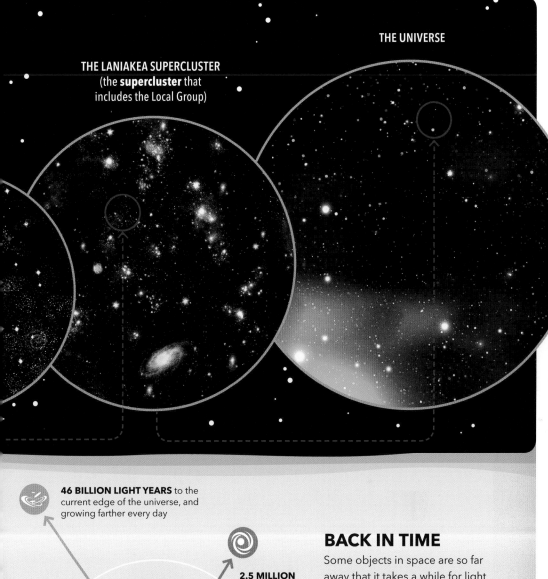

THE UNIVERSE

THE LANIAKEA SUPERCLUSTER
(the **supercluster** that
includes the Local Group)

46 BILLION LIGHT YEARS to the
current edge of the universe, and
growing farther every day

**2.5 MILLION
LIGHT YEARS**
to Andromeda,
the closest
galaxy to the
Milky Way

DISTANCE FROM EARTH

4.22 LIGHT YEARS to
Proxima Centauri, the
closest star to the Sun

EARTH

8.3 LIGHT MINUTES
to the Sun

26,000 LIGHT YEARS
to the center of the
Milky Way

BACK IN TIME

Some objects in space are so far
away that it takes a while for light
reflected off of them to reach us.
When the light does reach us, we
see the object as it was when the
light reflected off it in the past. For
example, we see the Sun as it was
8.3 minutes ago, because this is
the amount of time it takes for light
to travel from the Sun to Earth. For
objects that are much farther away,
we see them as they were much
farther back in time.

THE BIG BANG

Most astronomers believe that the universe was created 13.8 billion years ago, after an explosion known as the Big Bang.

 ## THE THEORY

According to the Big Bang theory, the universe began as a single point. In a tiny fraction of a second, there was a giant explosion (the Big Bang) and hot **matter** and energy expanded from this single point. Over time, matter and energy spread out and cooled down. The universe has been expanding ever since.

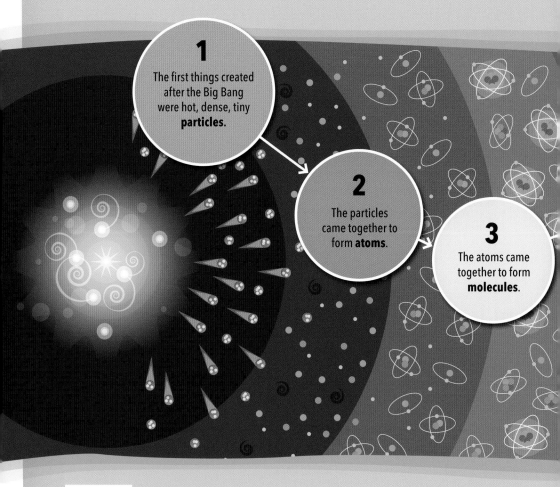

1

The first things created after the Big Bang were hot, dense, tiny **particles.**

2

The particles came together to form **atoms**.

3

The atoms came together to form **molecules**.

TIME

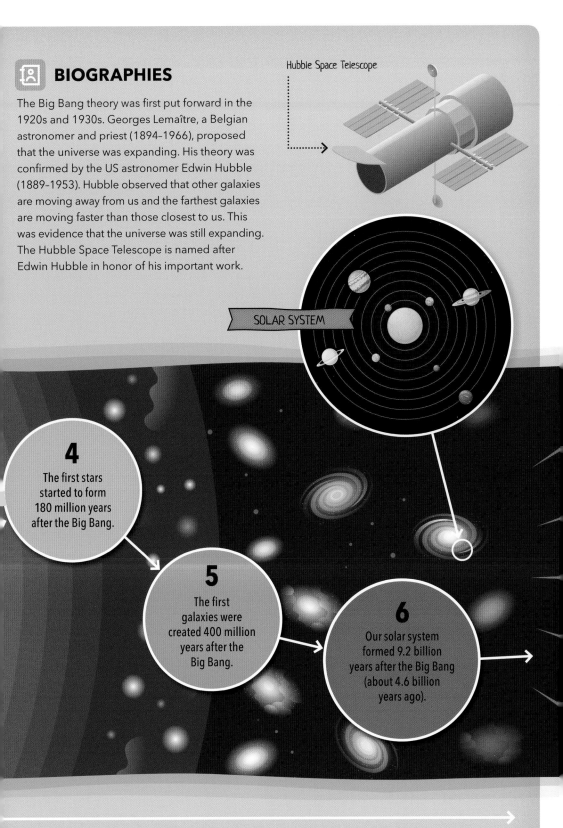

📇 BIOGRAPHIES

The Big Bang theory was first put forward in the 1920s and 1930s. Georges Lemaître, a Belgian astronomer and priest (1894–1966), proposed that the universe was expanding. His theory was confirmed by the US astronomer Edwin Hubble (1889–1953). Hubble observed that other galaxies are moving away from us and the farthest galaxies are moving faster than those closest to us. This was evidence that the universe was still expanding. The Hubble Space Telescope is named after Edwin Hubble in honor of his important work.

Hubble Space Telescope

SOLAR SYSTEM

4
The first stars started to form 180 million years after the Big Bang.

5
The first galaxies were created 400 million years after the Big Bang.

6
Our solar system formed 9.2 billion years after the Big Bang (about 4.6 billion years ago).

GO QUIZ YOURSELF!

1 How many planets are there in our solar system?

2 How far is Venus from the Sun?

3 What is a dwarf planet?

4 What is at the center of our solar system?

5 Where are most of the asteroids in our solar system?

6 Why is a year longer on Neptune than on Mars?

7 How long is a year on Mercury?

8 What is the Local Group?

9 How far is 1 AU in miles or kilometers?

10 How far is 1 light year in miles or kilometers?

11 How far is Earth from Proxima Centauri in light years?

12 How long does it take for light from the Sun to reach Earth?

13 How long ago was the universe created?

14 How long after the Big Bang did the first stars start to form?

15 When did our solar system form?

16 How did Georges Lemaître contribute to the Big Bang theory?

17 Which object is named after Edwin Hubble?

THE INNER PLANETS

MERCURY

★ Mercury is 2.6 times smaller than Earth (only slightly larger than the Moon).

★ On Mercury, the Sun would appear three times larger in the sky than it does on Earth.

★ Mercury spins on its **axis** very slowly. One day on Mercury is equivalent to 58.7 Earth days!

EARTH

(see pages 14–15)

VENUS

★ Venus is 1.1 times smaller than Earth.

★ Venus is the hottest planet in the solar system. Its thick **atmosphere** traps heat from the Sun.

★ Unlike most planets, Venus spins clockwise. This means that the Sun rises in the west and sets in the east.

MARS

★ Mars is 1.9 times smaller than Earth.

★ Mars' red color comes from rust (iron oxide) in its soil.

★ Wind on Mars is so strong that occasionally, dust storms form that cover the whole planet.

EXPLORING MARS

1965
The first close-up photos of Mars were taken by NASA's Mariner 4 spacecraft.

1976
The Viking 1 and 2 spacecraft landed on the surface of Mars.

1997
Sojourner was the first wheeled **rover** to explore the surface of another planet when it visited Mars.

ROCKY PLANETS

The inner planets are known as rocky planets because they are made of rock and metal. Their **cores** (centers) are made of metal, surrounded by a rocky **mantle**. The mantle is covered with a solid outer **crust**.

MANTLE AND CRUST—249 MILES (401 KM) THICK

STRUCTURE OF MERCURY

CORE—1,289 MILES (2,074 KM) RADIUS

Mercury has an unusually large core and a thin mantle. This may be because the outer layers of its mantle were chipped away when the planet crashed into other objects during the formation of the solar system.

SURFACE

Rocky planets often have craters and volcanoes. Craters form when **meteoroids** and comets hit the surface. Volcanoes are created by **molten** rock rising from the mantle to the surface of the planet. Venus has tens of thousands of volcanoes. Mars is home to Olympus Mons, which is the largest volcano in the solar system that we know about. At 15.5 miles (25 km) high, it is three times taller than Mount Everest.

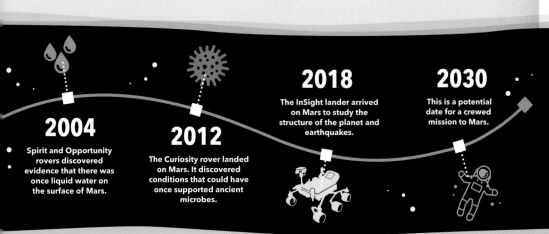

2018
The InSight lander arrived on Mars to study the structure of the planet and earthquakes.

2030
This is a potential date for a crewed mission to Mars.

2004
Spirit and Opportunity rovers discovered evidence that there was once liquid water on the surface of Mars.

2012
The Curiosity rover landed on Mars. It discovered conditions that could have once supported ancient microbes.

EARTH

Earth is our home planet and the only planet in the universe known to contain life. It is a rocky planet, which is mainly covered in water.

diameter **7917.5 miles (12,742 km)**

age **4.54 billion years**

 surface area covered by water **71%**

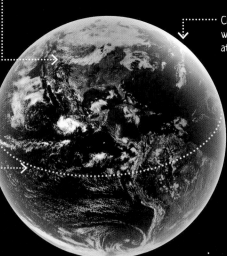

The land on Earth is formed of seven continents, which can be seen from space.

Clouds, made from drops of water or ice, form in the atmosphere around Earth.

Earth's circumference at its widest part, the equator (an imaginary line around the middle of the planet), is 24,901 miles (40,074 km).

The Moon is the only other body in space that humans have visited, apart from Earth.

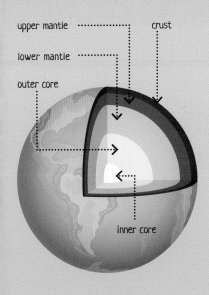

upper mantle

lower mantle

outer core

crust

inner core

STRUCTURE

Earth is made up of five main layers.

The inner core is a solid sphere of nickel and iron. It is the hottest layer, with temperatures reaching up to 9,752 °F (5,400 °C). It measures 1,517 miles (2,442 km) in diameter.

The outer core surrounds the inner core. It is made of liquid iron and nickel and is around 1,429 miles (2,300 km) thick.

The thickest layer is the mantle. It can be divided into two parts: the upper mantle and the lower mantle. Heat from the core melts rock in the mantle and makes it move toward the crust.

The crust is the outer layer. It is 19 miles (30 km) thick on land and about 1.9 miles (3 km) thick under the ocean.

ATMOSPHERE

Earth is surrounded by an atmosphere made up of 78 percent nitrogen, 21 percent **oxygen**, and 1 percent other gases, such as **carbon dioxide**. The atmosphere protects the planet from radiation from the Sun. Many small space rocks (meteoroids) burn up in the atmosphere, but some make it through and fall to Earth as **meteorites**.

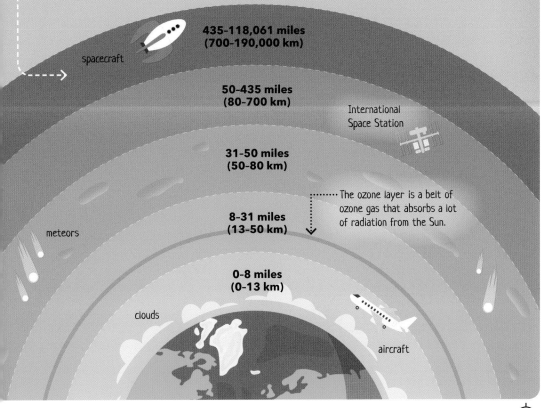

spacecraft

435–118,061 miles (700–190,000 km)

50–435 miles (80–700 km)

International Space Station

31–50 miles (50–80 km)

The ozone layer is a belt of ozone gas that absorbs a lot of radiation from the Sun.

8–31 miles (13–50 km)

meteors

0–8 miles (0–13 km)

clouds

aircraft

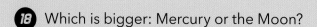
18 Which is bigger: Mercury or the Moon?

19 How long is one day on Mercury in Earth days?

20 Why is Venus the hottest planet in the solar system?

21 In which direction does Venus spin?

22 Why does Mars look red?

23 What are the cores of the rocky planets made of?

24 What is the largest known volcano in the solar system?

25 Name an important discovery that rovers have made on Mars.

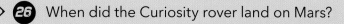

26 When did the Curiosity rover land on Mars?

27 How old is Earth?

28 How much of Earth is covered in water?

29 How many continents are there on Earth?

30 Apart from Earth, what is the only other body in space that humans have visited?

31 Which is the hottest layer of Earth's structure?

32 Is Earth's crust thicker on land or under the ocean?

33 What is the name for a small space rock that falls to Earth?

34 Name two gases in Earth's atmosphere.

THE ASTEROID BELT

Most of the asteroids in our solar system are found in a giant belt between Mars and Jupiter. They are left over from the formation of the solar system.

THE ASTEROID BELT CONTAINS:

1 dwarf planet, Ceres

1.1–1.9 million asteroids larger than 0.6 miles (1 km) in diameter

millions of smaller asteroids

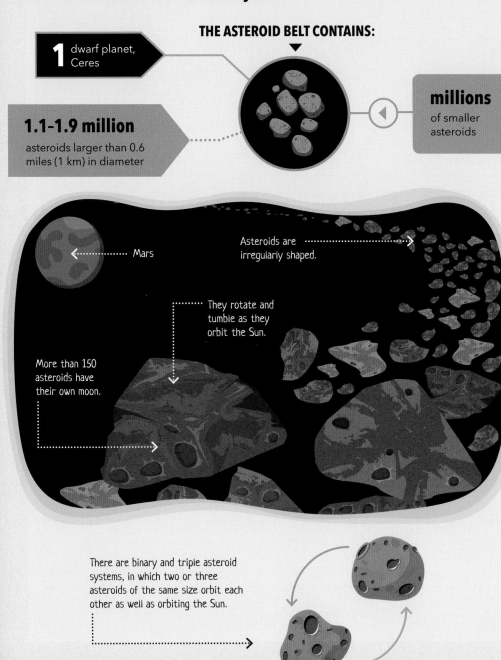

Mars

Asteroids are irregularly shaped.

They rotate and tumble as they orbit the Sun.

More than 150 asteroids have their own moon.

There are binary and triple asteroid systems, in which two or three asteroids of the same size orbit each other as well as orbiting the Sun.

HISTORY

During the formation of the solar system, Jupiter's strong gravitational pull started to attract nearby matter. This made it impossible for any planets to get larger. Its gravity caused the small planets in the area to crash into each other and break down into asteroids, forming the asteroid belt.

OFF COURSE

Gravity from Jupiter and Mars can change an asteroid's orbit and send some of them flying off into space. In the past, asteroids and asteroid fragments crashed into Earth and many other planets. These impacts caused huge geological and environmental changes. Many scientists believe that a giant asteroid collision on Earth led to the extinction of most of the dinosaurs.

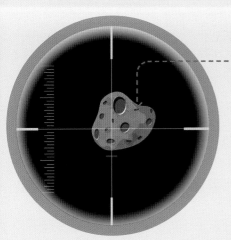

NEAR-EARTH ASTEROIDS

Near-Earth Asteroids (NEA) are asteroids outside of the asteroid belt whose orbits come close to Earth. In the future, it may be possible for us to extract resources, such as metal and rock, from some of them. Astronomers are developing plans to deal with NEA that could potentially crash into Earth, but the risk of collision is low.

THE OUTER PLANETS

Jupiter, Saturn, Uranus, and Neptune are the farthest planets from the Sun in our solar system. Their distance makes it harder for us to study them, but various spacecraft have flown past to make observations.

JUPITER

★ Jupiter is 11 times larger than Earth.

★ The stripes that we see on Jupiter are clouds of ammonia and water.

★ Jupiter is twice as massive as all of the other planets combined.

URANUS

★ Uranus is 4 times larger than Earth.

★ Clouds on Uranus smell like rotten eggs because they contain hydrogen sulfide gas.

★ Uranus rotates clockwise on its side around a horizontal axis rather than a vertical axis, like the other planets. This may be because of a collision with a large planet a long time ago.

SATURN

★ Saturn is 9.1 times larger than Earth.

★ More than 60 moons orbit Saturn.

★ Saturn's **density** is less than water, so it could float in a bathtub, if there was one big enough!

NEPTUNE

★ Neptune is 3.9 times larger than Earth.

★ Neptune is the windiest planet in the solar system, with some winds at speeds of 1,243 mph (2,000 kph).

★ Neptune's blue color comes from methane in its atmosphere.

GIANT PLANETS

Jupiter and Saturn are gas giants. The outer layers of the planets are made up of gas, probably formed around a solid core. This means they have no defined surface, so no spacecraft could land on them. Uranus and Neptune are ice giants. They have rocky cores, surrounded by layers of thick, icy, soupy materials.

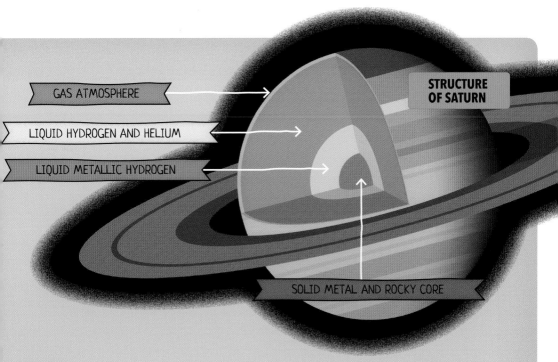

GAS ATMOSPHERE

LIQUID HYDROGEN AND HELIUM

LIQUID METALLIC HYDROGEN

SOLID METAL AND ROCKY CORE

RINGS

Saturn is well-known for its rings, but all of the outer planets actually have rings, although some are hard to see. Saturn's rings are made up of dust and pieces of ice and rock.

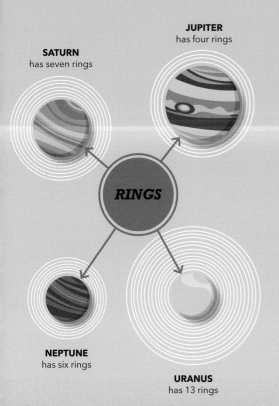

JUPITER
has four rings

SATURN
has seven rings

RINGS

NEPTUNE
has six rings

URANUS
has 13 rings

THE GREAT RED SPOT

The Great Red Spot on Jupiter is actually a giant hurricane that is larger than Earth.

It takes six days for the hurricane to spin around once.

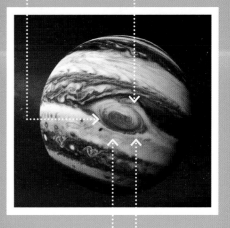

Winds in the hurricane move at more than 398 mph (640 kph).

The storm has been raging for more than 150 years.

GO QUIZ YOURSELF!

35 How many asteroids in the asteroid belt have their own moon?

36 Which dwarf planet is in the asteroid belt?

37 What kind of shape do asteroids have?

38 What is a binary asteroid system?

39 What makes asteroids change orbit?

40 What may have been caused by an asteroid crash on Earth?

41 What are NEA?

42 Which outer planet is the largest?

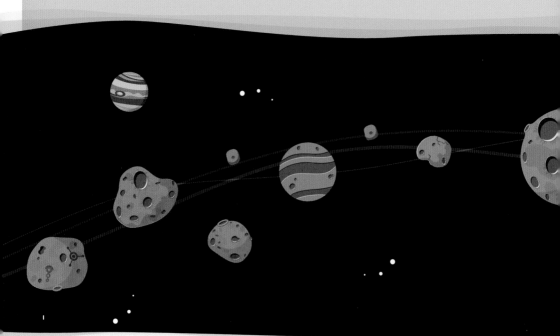

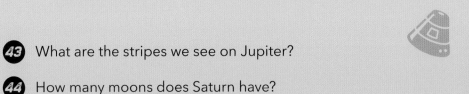

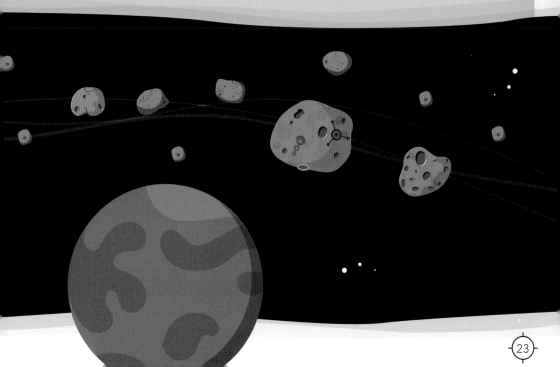

THE SUN

The Sun provides light and heat to Earth and other planets. It is the largest and heaviest object in the solar system.

THE SUN IN NUMBERS

99.8%: the amount of mass in the solar system made up by the Sun

1.3 MILLION: the number of Earths that could fit inside the Sun

6.5 BILLION: the number of years the Sun is expected to last before becoming a white dwarf (see page 37)

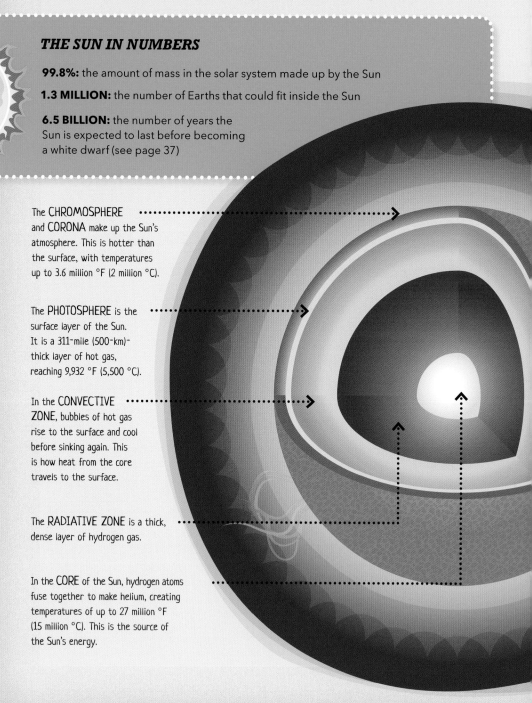

The CHROMOSPHERE and CORONA make up the Sun's atmosphere. This is hotter than the surface, with temperatures up to 3.6 million °F (2 million °C).

The PHOTOSPHERE is the surface layer of the Sun. It is a 311-mile (500-km)- thick layer of hot gas, reaching 9,932 °F (5,500 °C).

In the CONVECTIVE ZONE, bubbles of hot gas rise to the surface and cool before sinking again. This is how heat from the core travels to the surface.

The RADIATIVE ZONE is a thick, dense layer of hydrogen gas.

In the CORE of the Sun, hydrogen atoms fuse together to make helium, creating temperatures of up to 27 million °F (15 million °C). This is the source of the Sun's energy.

COMPOSITION

The Sun is currently made up of this amount of hydrogen, helium, and other elements. Eventually all of the hydrogen will be turned into helium and the Sun will change form (see pages 36-37).

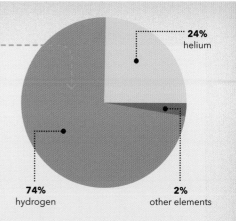

24%
helium

74%
hydrogen

2%
other elements

SUNSPOTS are dark patches on the surface that are cooler than the area around them.

A PROMINENCE is a loop of gas that comes off the surface of the Sun.

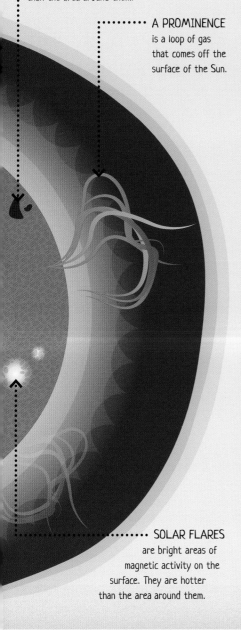

SOLAR FLARES are bright areas of magnetic activity on the surface. They are hotter than the area around them.

UNDERSTANDING THE SUN

In 150 CE, the ancient Greek astronomer Ptolomy (100-170 CE) suggested Earth was at the center of the solar system and the Sun orbited around it. This idea was accepted until the sixteenth century, when the astronomer Nicolaus Copernicus (1473-1543) published a book suggesting the Sun was actually at the center of the solar system. This was a huge advance in science. Many future astronomers, such as Galileo Galilei (1564-1642), went on to base new pioneering work on Copernicus's ideas.

In Ptolmy's geocentric model, Earth is at the center of the solar system.

In Copernicus's heliocentric model, the Sun is at the center of the solar system.

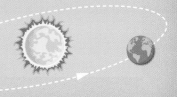

THE SUN ON EARTH

The Sun makes life on Earth possible. Our distance from the Sun means that our planet isn't too hot or cold. The Sun also affects Earth in other ways, causing day and night and the seasons.

TEMPERATURES ON EARTH IF THE SUN DISAPPEARED

57 °F (14 °C)

Average temperature with the Sun

-0.4 °F (-18 °C)

Average temperature without the Sun (after 1 week)

-99 °F (-73 °C)

Average temperature without the Sun (after 1 year)

-400 °F (-240 °C)

Average temperature without the Sun (after millions of years)

DAY AND NIGHT

Earth spins counterclockwise on its axis as it goes around the Sun. It takes 24 hours to spin once, so this is the length of an Earth day. The side facing the Sun experiences daytime, receiving light and heat from the Sun. The side facing away from the Sun experiences night time, which is dark and colder.

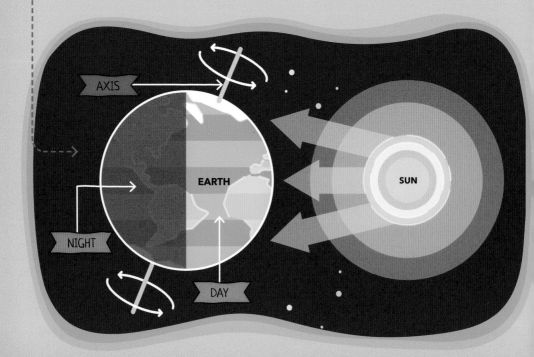

AXIS

EARTH

NIGHT

DAY

SUN

SEASONS

Earth is tilted on its axis by 23.5 degrees. This means that different parts of Earth are closer to the Sun at different times of the year. This creates seasons. The **hemisphere** that is tilted toward the Sun experiences summer, while the other hemisphere that is tilted away from the Sun experiences winter.

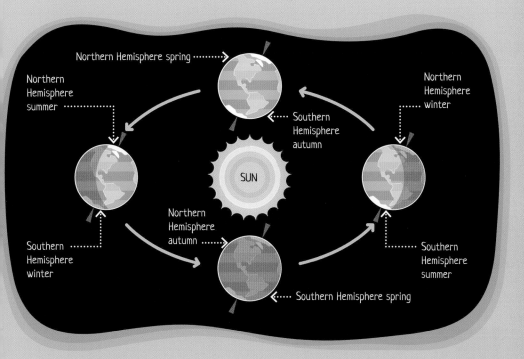

Northern Hemisphere spring

Northern Hemisphere summer

Northern Hemisphere winter

Southern Hemisphere autumn

SUN

Northern Hemisphere autumn

Southern Hemisphere winter

Southern Hemisphere summer

Southern Hemisphere spring

ECLIPSES

Occasionally, the Moon moves between the Sun and Earth. It blocks the light from the Sun and casts a shadow on Earth. For a few minutes, the Sun disappears and there is no light. This is known as a total **solar eclipse**. They are unusual, because the Moon is rarely in the exact position to totally cover the shape of the Sun in the sky.

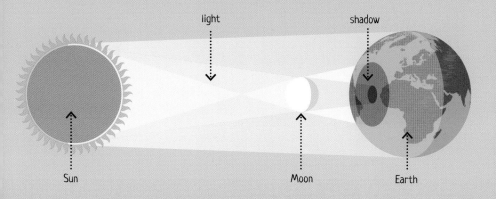

light

shadow

Sun

Moon

Earth

GO QUIZ YOURSELF!

52 How many Earths could fit inside the Sun?

53 How many years will it be before the Sun changes into a white dwarf?

54 How hot is the Sun's atmosphere?

55 What happens in the core of the Sun?

56 How does heat from the Sun's core travel to the surface?

57 How hot is the surface of the Sun?

58 What is a sunspot?

59 What is the name for a bright area of magnetic activity on the surface of the Sun?

60 Which two main gases is the Sun made up of?

61 Who suggested Earth was at the center of the solar system?

62 Who suggested the Sun was at the center of the solar system?

63 What is the average temperature on Earth, thanks to the Sun?

64 What would happen to the temperature on Earth if the Sun disappeared?

65 How long does it take for Earth to spin once on its axis?

66 Why do seasons exist on Earth?

67 When it is summer in the Southern Hemisphere, which season is it in the Northern Hemisphere?

68 What causes a total solar eclipse?

THE MOON

A moon is a body in space that orbits a planet. Earth has one moon. Earth's Moon is the fifth-largest moon in our solar system.

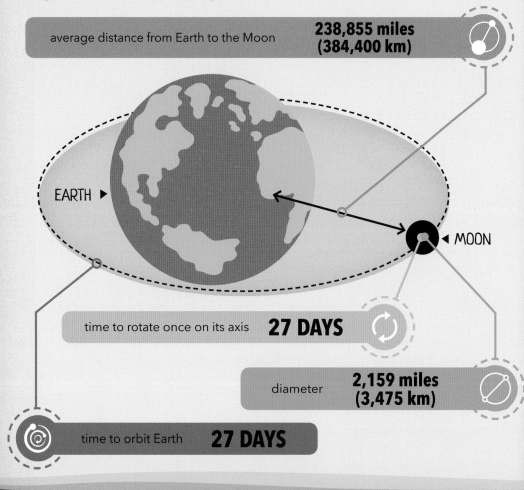

average distance from Earth to the Moon **238,855 miles (384,400 km)**

EARTH ▶

◀ MOON

time to rotate once on its axis **27 DAYS**

diameter **2,159 miles (3,475 km)**

time to orbit Earth **27 DAYS**

PHASES

The shape of the Moon appears to change throughout the month. This is because different parts of the Moon are lit up by sunlight as it moves through its orbit.

In a new moon, sunlight is hitting the back half of the Moon that is not visible.

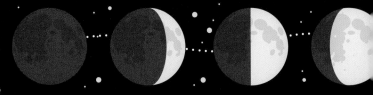

NEW MOON   WAXING CRESCENT   FIRST QUARTER   WAXING GIBB

ANCIENT SCARS

The Moon's surface is covered in craters. These are deep depressions left behind by space rocks that have been pulled into the Moon's orbit and have crashed into the surface at great speeds.

The dark areas on the surface of the Moon are known as lunar maria (singular: mare). They are flat plains covered in a dark rock called basalt. They were formed by ancient volcanic eruptions.

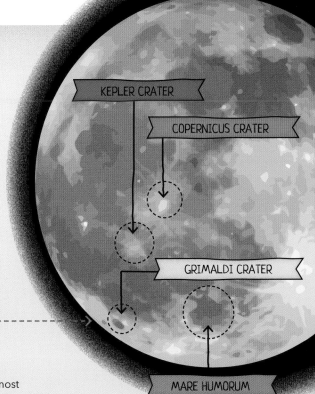

KEPLER CRATER

COPERNICUS CRATER

GRIMALDI CRATER

MARE HUMORUM

TIDES

Every day on Earth, the sea level along most coasts rises and falls. These changes are known as tides. They are caused by gravity, an invisible force that pulls objects together. When the Moon's gravity pulls on Earth, it drags ocean water toward the Moon, and the sea level rises. This is called a high tide. The opposite side of Earth also experiences a high tide. This is because the movement of the Moon makes Earth shake slightly and flings water toward the other side of the planet. As Earth spins on its axis, the side facing the Moon changes and different parts of Earth get high and low tides. Gravity from the Sun also affects tides on Earth.

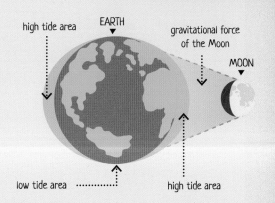

high tide area   EARTH ▼   gravitational force of the Moon

MOON ▼

low tide area   high tide area

In a full moon, sunlight hits the entire half of the Moon that is facing Earth.

FULL MOON   WANING GIBBOUS   LAST QUARTER   WANING CRESCENT   NEW MOON

MOON EXPLORATION

The Space Race was a competition in the 1900s between the USA and the Soviet Union (USSR) to see which country would be the first to send a person into space.

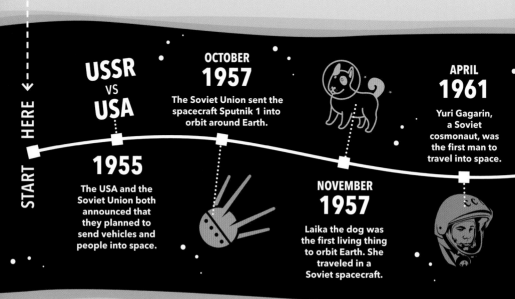

START HERE

USSR vs **USA**

OCTOBER 1957
The Soviet Union sent the spacecraft Sputnik 1 into orbit around Earth.

APRIL 1961
Yuri Gagarin, a Soviet cosmonaut, was the first man to travel into space.

1955
The USA and the Soviet Union both announced that they planned to send vehicles and people into space.

NOVEMBER 1957
Laika the dog was the first living thing to orbit Earth. She traveled in a Soviet spacecraft.

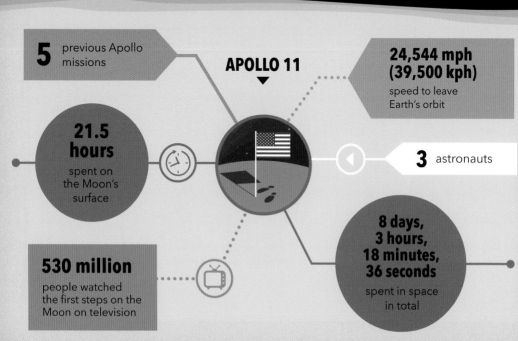

5 previous Apollo missions

APOLLO 11

24,544 mph (39,500 kph)
speed to leave Earth's orbit

21.5 hours
spent on the Moon's surface

3 astronauts

530 million
people watched the first steps on the Moon on television

8 days, 3 hours, 18 minutes, 36 seconds
spent in space in total

NEIL ARMSTRONG

Neil Armstrong (1930–2012) was an American astronaut. He worked as a test pilot for NASA before becoming an astronaut. Armstrong went through difficult tests and experiments to prove he was prepared for the demands of space travel.

He first travelled into space on the Gemini 8 mission in 1966. In 1969, he led the Apollo 11 mission to the Moon. He was the first person to set foot on the Moon. After that, Armstrong became a worldwide celebrity. He was given many medals.

JUNE
1963
The Soviet cosmonaut Valentina Tereshkova was the first woman to travel into space.

FEBRUARY
1966
Luna 9, launched by the Soviet Union, was the first spacecraft to land on the Moon.

JULY
1969
Neil Armstrong and Buzz Aldrin, American astronauts from the Apollo 11 mission, were the first humans to walk on the Moon.

MARCH
1965
Alexei Leonov, a Soviet cosmonaut, was the first person to leave a spacecraft in space and perform a spacewalk (EVA).

1967
NASA started training astronauts and practices for a Moon landing with several Apollo missions.

BACK TO THE MOON

After Apollo 11, NASA astronauts landed on the Moon five more times. They explored the surface in rovers and collected hundreds of pounds of rocks and soil to be studied back on Earth. The last crewed trip to the Moon was in 1972. Since then, some countries have sent robotic rovers to the Moon and there are plans for more crewed missions in the future.

Armstrong and Aldrin traveled down to the surface of the Moon in the *Eagle* lunar module.

The astronauts carried out experiments and collected rock and dust samples.

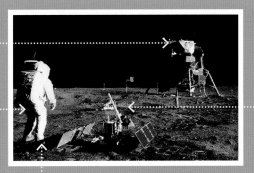

Protective spacesuits kept the astronauts safe and warm.

Oxygen was pumped into the suits so they could breathe.

GO QUIZ YOURSELF!

69 What's the average distance between Earth and the Moon?

70 What is the diameter of the Moon?

71 How long does it take for the Moon to orbit Earth?

72 What does the first quarter of the Moon look like?

73 How were craters created on the Moon?

74 Which rock covers the flat plains on the Moon?

75 Which force causes tides?

76 Which other body in the solar system affects tides on Earth?

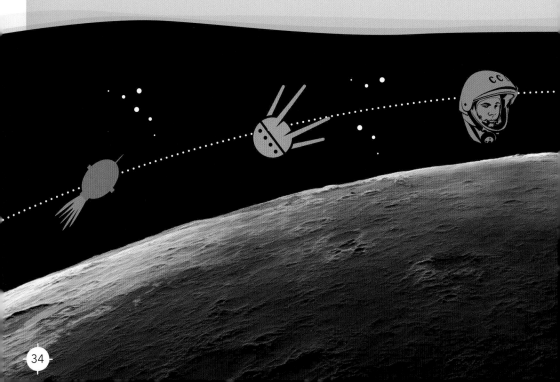

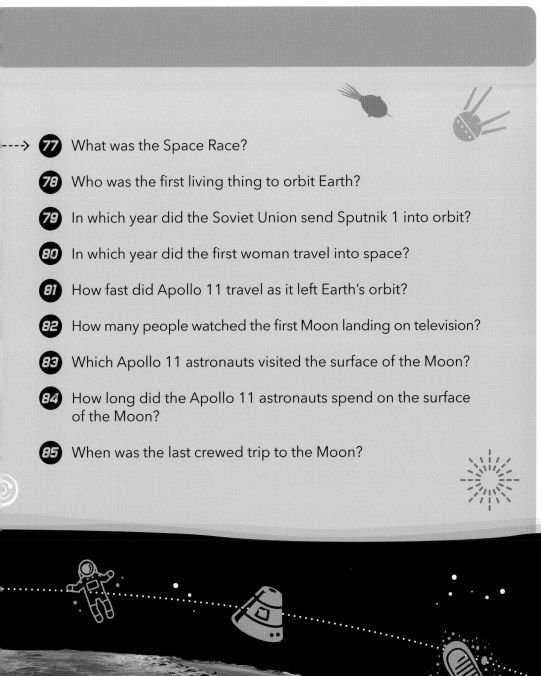

77 What was the Space Race?

78 Who was the first living thing to orbit Earth?

79 In which year did the Soviet Union send Sputnik 1 into orbit?

80 In which year did the first woman travel into space?

81 How fast did Apollo 11 travel as it left Earth's orbit?

82 How many people watched the first Moon landing on television?

83 Which Apollo 11 astronauts visited the surface of the Moon?

84 How long did the Apollo 11 astronauts spend on the surface of the Moon?

85 When was the last crewed trip to the Moon?

STARS

Stars are huge balls of very hot gas. Their size, brightness, color, and temperature depend on their phase in their life cycle.

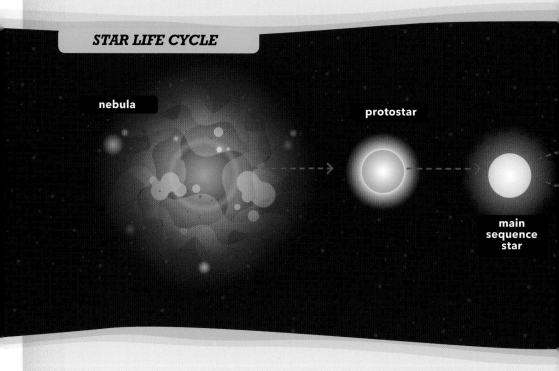

STAR LIFE CYCLE

nebula

protostar

main sequence star

Nebulae
Stars begin their life in a **nebula**—a massive cloud of dust and hydrogen gas. Over time, gravity slowly begins to pull the dust and gas together to form a clump.

Protostar
When the clump of dust and gas gets bigger, it will eventually collapse under the weight of its own gravity. This causes it to heat up. **Nuclear fusion** begins as parts of the hydrogen atoms join together to make helium. This produces energy and makes the core of the star even hotter.

Main sequence star
This is the most stable phase in the life of a star. Our Sun is currently in this stage and will be for billions of years. The pressure of the reactions deep in the core is balanced by the gravity that holds the star together. The energy from nuclear fusion makes the star glow.

950 the number of times larger that the star Betelgeuse is than the Sun, making it one of the largest known stars

2,000-2,500 the number of stars a person with good eyesight could see in the night sky.

Red giant

When all of the hydrogen in a star has been turned into helium, the star becomes unstable. It expands and begins to glow red. This will eventually happen to the Sun. Stars larger than the Sun turn into red super giants, which are much bigger than red giants.

White dwarf

Eventually, red giants become smaller because of the force of gravity pulling inward. They fade and turn white as they cool down.

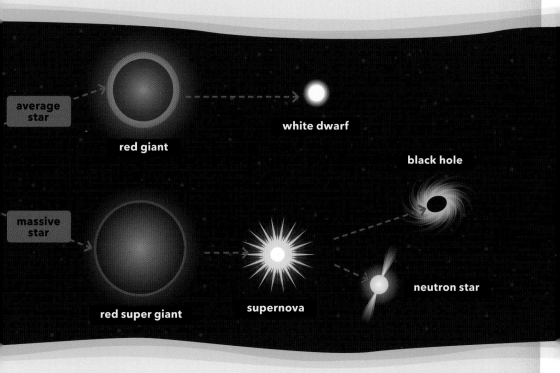

average star

red giant

white dwarf

black hole

massive star

red super giant

supernova

neutron star

Supernova

Stars that are bigger than the Sun will keep getting hotter and larger as more of their hydrogen turns to helium. They turn into red super giants. When the core of a red super giant collapses, it explodes as a supernova.

Black hole

A supernova can leave behind a black hole, which attracts and pulls in matter and energy (see page 42).

Neutron star

Supernovas can also leave behind neutron stars. This is the collapsed core of a star. They are small, but very dense.

TWINKLE, TWINKLE

Stars appear to twinkle in the sky. This is actually an effect caused by Earth's atmosphere, rather than the star itself. As rays of light move through gases of different densities in the atmosphere, they move very slightly to the side. To the eye, this movement makes it look as though the star is twinkling.

GALAXIES

A galaxy is a collection of stars, gas, and dust held together by gravity.

THE MILKY WAY

Our Sun and solar system are in the Milky Way galaxy. This galaxy also contains about 200 billion other stars. The Milky Way galaxy has a spiral shape with several arms and spurs. Our solar system is located in the Orion Spur.

There is a supermassive black hole at the center of the Milky Way, but it has never been seen.

Perseus Arm

Orion Spur

GALAXY TYPES

There are many other galaxies across the universe besides our own. Other galaxies have different shapes. Some are elliptical (smooth and oval shaped), while others are irregular (blob shaped).

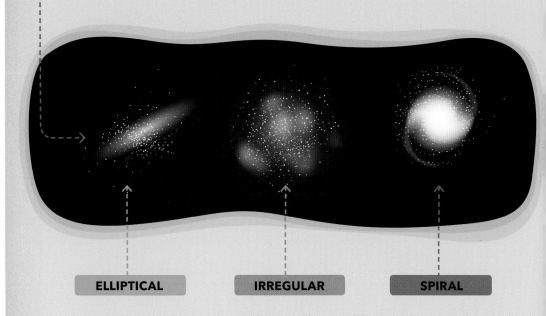

ELLIPTICAL

IRREGULAR

SPIRAL

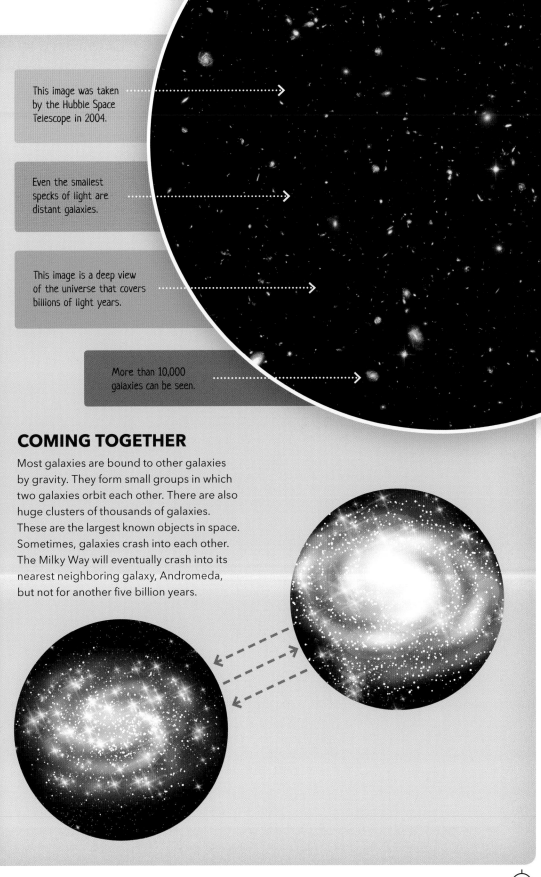

This image was taken by the Hubble Space Telescope in 2004.

Even the smallest specks of light are distant galaxies.

This image is a deep view of the universe that covers billions of light years.

More than 10,000 galaxies can be seen.

COMING TOGETHER

Most galaxies are bound to other galaxies by gravity. They form small groups in which two galaxies orbit each other. There are also huge clusters of thousands of galaxies. These are the largest known objects in space. Sometimes, galaxies crash into each other. The Milky Way will eventually crash into its nearest neighboring galaxy, Andromeda, but not for another five billion years.

GO QUIZ YOURSELF!

86 What is a nebula?

87 Which is the most stable phase in the life of a star?

88 Which phase is the Sun currently in?

89 Why do stars glow?

90 Which phase comes first in the life cycle of a star: the red giant or white dwarf?

91 Which stars turn into red super giants?

92 Name one thing that a supernova explosion can leave behind.

93 Which star is 950 times larger than the Sun?

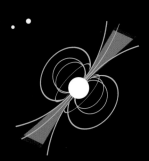

- - - →

94 How many stars can a person with good eyesight see in the night sky?

95 What is a neutron star?

96 Why do stars appear to twinkle in the sky?

97 How many other stars are in the Milky Way?

98 On which spur of the Milky Way is our solar system located?

99 What is at the center of the Milky Way?

100 Name the three shapes of galaxies.

101 What is our nearest neighboring galaxy?

102 When will the Milky Way crash into its nearest neighboring galaxy?

SPACE ODDITIES

Space is filled with amazing objects with incredible features. Every year, astronomers learn more about these space oddities and discover even stranger objects in space.

BLACK HOLES

A black hole is a huge amount of matter packed into a very small space. It has incredibly strong gravity—nothing can escape its pull, not even light. Supermassive black holes are found at the center of most galaxies. The center of a black hole can't be seen because it emits no light. However, we can figure out the location of a black hole by observing the effect of its gravity on nearby objects.

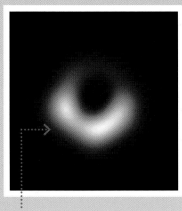

This photo shows the black hole at the center of the M87 galaxy. The ring of light is formed by light bending under the massive gravitational pull of the black hole. The black circle in the center isn't actually the black hole, because it can't be seen— it's the shadow of the black hole.

The center of a black hole is a single point.

Past this point, known as the event horizon, nothing can escape the pull of a black hole's gravity.

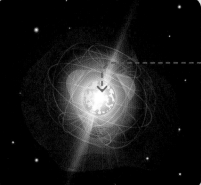

MAGNETARS

A magnetar is a type of neutron star (see page 37) with a very powerful magnetic field. Its magnetic field is one trillion times stronger than Earth's. The energy from a magnetar's field heats up its surface to nearly 18 million °F (10 million °C).

EXOPLANETS

Exoplanets are planets that orbit stars in other solar systems. Astronomers have observed 4,000 exoplanets so far, but there may be as many as a trillion in just the Milky Way. Conditions on exoplanets vary hugely.

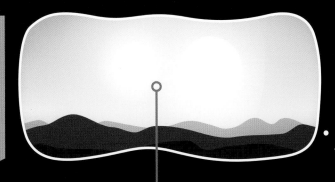

On 55 Cancri e,

the same side always faces its star, so temperatures can reach 4,352 °F (2,400 °C). On the opposite side, it's only 2,012 °F (1,100 °C).

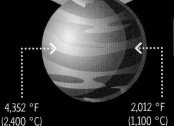

4,352 °F
(2,400 °C)

2,012 °F
(1,100 °C)

Kepler-16b

orbits two stars, so two "suns" set on the horizon.

TrES-2b

is the darkest planet ever discovered orbiting a star. However, it may not be pitch black on the surface because its burning atmosphere might glow red!

Gravity from **WASP-12's** star is stretching the shape of the planet from a sphere to an egg shape. Eventually, the planet will be absorbed into the star.

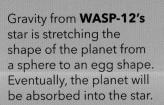

QUIZ TIME!

After you've finished testing yourself, why not use this book to make a quiz to test your friends and family? You could take questions from each section to make different rounds, or mix and match across the book for a general knowledge space quiz. You can even make up your own quiz questions! Use these space oddities facts to get you started. For example, **"What is an exoplanet?"** or **"How can you figure out the location of a black hole if you can't see it?"**

ANSWERS

1	8	36	Ceres
2	67.1 million miles (108 million km)	37	An irregular shape
3	Round objects that orbit the Sun, which are smaller than planets but don't have enough gravity to clear their orbit path of smaller objects	38	Two asteroids that orbit each other as well as the Sun
		39	Gravity from other planets, such as Jupiter or Mars
4	The Sun	40	The extinction of most of the dinosaurs
5	In the asteroid belt between Mars and Jupiter	41	Near-Earth Asteroids
		42	Jupiter
6	Because Neptune is farther from the Sun than Mars, so its orbit takes longer	43	Clouds of ammonia and water
		44	More than 60 moons
7	88 days	45	Uranus
8	The cluster of galaxies where the Milky Way is located	46	Because of methane in its atmosphere
		47	Because the outer layers of Jupiter are made of gas, so it doesn't have a solid surface
9	92,955,808 miles (149,597,871 km)		
10	Around 5.6 trillion miles (9 trillion km)	48	Uranus and Neptune
11	4.22 light years	49	A giant hurricane on Jupiter
12	8.3 (light) minutes	50	Dust and pieces of ice and rock
13	13.8 billion years ago	51	13
14	180 million years	52	1.3 million
15	About 4.6 billion years ago (9.2 billion years after the Big Bang)	53	6.5 billion years
		54	3.6 million °F (2 million °C)
16	He proposed that the universe was expanding	55	Hydrogen atoms fuse together to make helium
		56	Bubbles of hot gas rise from deep in the Sun out toward the surface
17	The Hubble Space Telescope		
18	Mercury	57	9,932 °F (5,500 °C)
19	58.7 Earth days	58	A dark patch on the surface of the Sun that is cooler than the area around it
20	Its thick atmosphere traps heat from the Sun		
		59	A solar flare
21	Clockwise	60	Hydrogen and helium
22	Because of rust (iron oxide) in its soil	61	Ptolemy, the ancient Greek astronomer
23	Metal	62	Nicolaus Copernicus
24	Olympus Mons	63	Around 57 °F (14 °C)
25	There once was liquid water on its surface and there were conditions that could once have supported ancient microbes	64	It would get much colder
		65	24 hours
		66	Because Earth is tilted on its axis, making some parts of the planet closer to the Sun at certain times of year
26	2012		
27	4.54 billion years old		
28	71 percent	67	Winter
29	Seven	68	The Moon moves between the Sun and Earth, blocks the light from the Sun, and casts a shadow on Earth
30	The Moon		
31	The inner core		
32	On land (19 miles (30 km), compared to 1.9 miles (3 km) under the ocean)	69	238,855 miles (384,400 km)
		70	2,159 miles (3,475 km)
33	A meteorite	71	27 days
34	Nitrogen, oxygen, carbon dioxide		
35	More than 150		

72 The left half of the Moon is dark, while the right half is light
73 By space rocks that were pulled into the Moon's orbit and crashed into the surface at great speeds
74 Basalt
75 Gravity
76 The Sun
77 A competition between the USA and the Soviet Union to see who would be the first to send a person into space
78 Laika the dog
79 1957
80 1963
81 24,544 mph (39,500 kph)
82 530 million
83 Neil Armstrong and Buzz Aldrin
84 21.5 hours
85 1972
86 A massive cloud of dust and hydrogen gas where stars are born
87 Main sequence star
88 Main sequence star
89 Because of energy from nuclear fusion
90 Red giant
91 Stars that are larger than the Sun
92 A black hole or a neutron star
93 Betelgeuse
94 2,000–2,500 stars
95 The small, dense collapsed core of a star
96 Because light rays from stars shift position slightly as they pass through gases of different densities in Earth's atmosphere
97 About 200 billion
98 The Orion Spur
99 A supermassive black hole
100 Spiral, elliptical, irregular
101 The Andromeda galaxy
102 In about five billion years

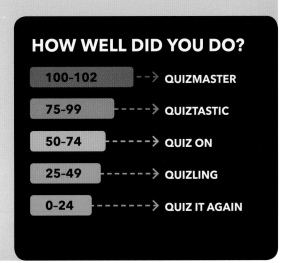

HOW WELL DID YOU DO?

100-102	-->	**QUIZMASTER**
75-99	---->	**QUIZTASTIC**
50-74	----->	**QUIZ ON**
25-49	------>	**QUIZLING**
0-24	------->	**QUIZ IT AGAIN**

GLOSSARY

asteroid A space rock that orbits the Sun

atmosphere The gases that surround Earth and other planets

atoms The smallest possible units of a substance

axis An imaginary straight line that goes through the center of a spinning object

carbon dioxide A gas that is released by burning fossil fuels or when humans and other animals breathe out

cluster A group of galaxies

cores The central parts of something

crust The outer layer of a planet

density The amount of mass a substance has compared to its size

dwarf planets Round objects that orbit the Sun, and are smaller than a planet but don't have enough gravity to attract objects in their orbit path

exoplanets Planets that orbit stars in other solar systems

gravity A force that pulls things toward each other

hemisphere One half of a planet

light year The distance that light travels in a year—roughly 5.9 trillion miles (9.5 trillion km)

mantle The part of a planet that surrounds the core and is under the crust

matter A physical substance in the universe

meteorite A small space rock that falls to the surface of a planet or a moon

meteoroids Small space rocks

molecules Groups of two or more atoms

molten In a liquid state

nebula A cloud of dust and hydrogen gas where stars are created

nuclear fusion When hydrogen atoms come together to make helium

orbit To travel around a planet or a star in a curved path

oxygen A gas that humans and other living things need to breathe to survive

particles Very small pieces of something

rover A small vehicle that can move over rough ground

solar eclipse When the Sun disappears from view on Earth because the Moon blocks its path

supercluster A very large group of smaller galaxy clusters

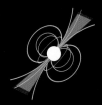

FURTHER INFORMATION

BOOKS

Becker, Helaine. *Everything Space: Blast Off for a Universe of Photos, Facts, and Fun!* National Geographic Kids, 2015.

DK. *Space: A visual encyclopedia.* DK Children, 2020.

Jefferis, David. Our Future in Space series. Crabtree Publishing, 2018.

Pettman, Kevin. *A Guide to Space.* Wayland, 2020.

WEBSITES

solarsystem.nasa.gov
Explore the solar system with this in-depth NASA guide.

hubblesite.org/images/gallery
See some of the most spectacular images of space ever taken by the Hubble Space Telescope.

https://kids.nationalgeographic.com/explore/space
Discover amazing facts and information about space.

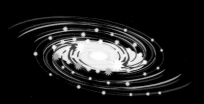

INDEX